This book is for JC

Winter Hands
First Edition 2007

ISBN: 978-0-905127-13-2

Cover design by Martin Chester

Published by
Shadowtrain Books
34 Pinewood Avenue
Carnforth
Lancaster
LA5 8AR
UK

http://shadowtrain.com

Acknowledgements:
Many thanks to the editors of the following, in which versions of these poems were first published:

A Combustible Edge (Bluechrome books)
The Big Picture (Lancaster Litfest)
Transmission
http://shadowtrain.com
www.stridemagazine.co.uk

Winter Hands

Contents

Fairground Man

dark hair curling round your ears, smell of generators and cigarettes and dirty denim, you open the door to my skin the ride of my life the holding on the screaming inside the slowly letting it out needing the breath of your sweat to take me in. you watch me as I circle you, and I am your dog on a string, your caravan.

cold staring towards the back of a field where later we might lie on trampled dandelions and stinging nettles, I imagine you taste of garlic and cumin and wood smoke, and with these blue lights tracing across my eyes, shouting go faster, your voice is the lashing of rain against a water drum.

calloused hands and rough broken skin, you call me darling as close to my ear as a man can be, your mouth a pile of damp leaves, your shoulders are burial mounds, your chest the bed of a river I want to get down on my knees and lean into.

take me into the dark of the field, where stars are below us in the stretching arms of streetlights, where dogs bark in the distance and my name is humming with engines.

Dislocated

you with your tin-can-to-hand love your bottle-neck love your ring-pull love while I sit silent I sit loud I sit crying in the bed with my angry love disturbed love me fighting you on the settee not moving me with backfire energy me bursting out me wanting to scream from my skin and you waiting watching you calm as light calm as washing as shoes and me wanting wildness wanting storm birds wanting hail and lightning you not noticing you listening to other sounds and me not opening my mouth but noise comes out like a weir me tumbling me falling down the stairs me with broken bones while you medicate the feeling of clouds and fields not even grass brushing you only a distant feeling almost as if you sense me scrambling over rocks this one gritstone the next a millstone me wanting to be sharpened me wanting to be crushed

Winter Hands

When she touches me I can forget. Her fingers freeze me on the chair. Eyes closed. No sounds reaching me.

She tugs at my jumper, my vest, the button of my jeans. I let her bite her nails into me, scrunch-close my eyes. A drip of sweat slips from her and sinks into the hollow of my collarbone. She trails her hair across my face. It smells of tangerine and cedar oil.

She mouths words into my belly, my pubic bone. She hums her wet hot mouth until she finishes me. It feels like a day, a month, a year and I am the skin of a frozen lake her tongue skates across.

Out of Practice with Words

I speak in notes, cross-firing messages against your door. You answer them in bridges. Wrap me in your clothes, I say, your shoes that are too big for me, your man-sized jackets. When you are quiet I will holdfast my breath, my eyes blind tight, I will speak to you in the language you teach me.

In the House of His Father

Inspired by Donald Rodney's photograph

~ 'In the House of My Father'

He held a house in the palm of his hand, a tiny house with broken windows and a caved-in roof. This was the house he grew up in, the house he'd wanted to feel safe in, made from the sickle-cell skin of his father. Skin walls, a skin roof, skin doors. He tried to repair it at night when his family thought he was sleeping, grafted it with skin peeled from his own body, fastened it with pins.

This was the house that held a thousand words, whispered in dry trembling voices that nobody else heard. He worried his breath might blow it away, that he might forget it was there, that his own hand might crush it.

In his dreams, there was a single light burning inside it, the flicker of a tea-light in the hallway.

Always in the morning it was gone, but he could smell the wax of burnt-out candles, feel the carbon stain of their wicks on his fingers.

He watched it shrivel and crack, his father's house, felt its skin-graft walls fall apart. But it was still hand-stitched to his own skin, held in the hollow of his palm.

Voices

His inside voices talked, chattered, shouted,

loud, LOUDER

I can't hear you I can't hear you voices.

Words running into words into words so he couldn't hear anything else, only a hundred different voices shouting over each other. Inside voices making a big inside-his-head deafening hum. He couldn't hear anything else. No thoughts. No outside noise. Only him. Listening to his own silence. Closing his eyes. Hearing his breath scream in out in out

his voices louder than their shouting

making their downstairs noise stop.

Music Divides Us

You don't understand it, he says. It's about rhythm, repetition. You have to get inside it. All that guitar music you like. That's a journey, music that makes you think. Where this is different. A space where you can stop thinking, or cut out the journey and still get to the same destination. And the beat takes you further into it so the rest of the world zones out and you're here in this place with patterns you can relate to. You have to understand, he says, it can take you outside yourself. It can make you feel safe.

Bruises

I laugh at first. The way you rub your hands against my thighs. You're sitting on my chest, knees in my armpits. It feels friendly, almost loving. But there's something in the way you look at me. Increasing the pressure.

Easy, I say, and you smile, watching my reaction as you press your fingers harder into me.

Bruises on my shoulder that I pretend are from doorframes, wardrobes, locker doors.

Key marks, thumb marks, finger-bruises that look like stairs.

I have a picture of you in my head, with your hair tied back looking oh so innocent, smiling in that sweet girl way. Hands slide into pockets. A nip and twist and gone, the ten second pain. I close my eyes, scrunch them up tight. I hear a low voice in my head. Save me.

I don't know who I'm talking to.

I want you. This is what you whisper. Nobody else, you say.

But it's menacing, hissed through clenched teeth, tight jaw, lips pressed tense together. Who would know the way you plead with me not to leave you?

I couldn't live without you. That's what you say.

Cover my face with a pillow. Press it down. Pull my hair. Dig your knuckles into my throat.

You

with your brown doe eyes lazy-blinking at me, smiling, calling me baby.

Nobody like you, you say

with your cute hips and your easy way of dressing, all denim and cotton, t-shirt too tight, waistband low-rise, and your black-eyed cat tattoo cut across the bottom of your back.

Sorry, you say, and maybe you mean it, maybe you don't.

I promise myself to stop you next time, hold you still, tell you that's enough. But part of me must be tied there with you, thinking I deserve it.

Hurt me, I think

hurt me.

I'm not brave enough to do it myself.

These Things Happened

walked like a woman with broken heels across pavements
bags trailing with open zips, hair splitting with braids
scuff-eyed and frozen with bruises rich as honey
with hands grazed along knuckles from punching drunk
on the backs of garages when you weren't watching
when you were busy with your lips on a cold neck
a shoulder, a face almost pinned to your collar
my skin scraped blue and without thought or reason
to confront you I became the colour of rain

stole leaves from sycamore trees
ripped them from branches and rubbed them like balm
into my cuts, into the dark nettle of these sores
until they stung like wasps and scarred my bones
they were friends these bandage and ointment days
they were winter lovers I held against my skin
under horsehair blankets, under mohair,
under wool nights I became a green song

later, washed in the ice and mud of puddles
scrubbed elbow to toe with pumice
and stones picked from disused quarries
leaving myself nine times at the edge

when you weren't watching
when you were sleeping
I became hard as gravel

Break Time

He takes me into the back of a wagon, a container he calls it, parked on the wasteland next to the mill. He says he wants me to hear the sounds inside, the echo of our voices, the clang clang.

Here, he says, offering his hands for me to stand on. There's a rough-burn rope tied to a handle and I pull myself up

metal box with its corrugated walls
no rolls of cloth or stuffing for mattresses or raw cotton, nothing but sheets of polythene we can lay down and roll in.

Close your eyes, he says putting his damp cotton hands over my face. Now listen.

I hear nothing - no wagons outside, no shuttle bang looms, no shouts as the shift changes.

Come closer, he says, wrapping his overall arms round my waist. He prickle-kisses my neck and his mouth is the warm of a steam pipe.

Dovecote

1.

The air heaves with the stench of moulted feathers. Hundreds of pigeons flap, over a thousand maybe, their wings beating against stone. The cooing nearly deafens me. It means I can't listen out for horseshoes clatting against the cobbles, or hear the scratch of rats in the yard, or squabs chirping in their nesting boxes or the sound of my own voice talking out loud, as I often do when I clear out the nests.

I like being in here, crouching under the lintel into the dark enclosed cote. It's like stepping inside myself. I climb the plinth steps, fix the ladder against the curved wall, and reach into the stone nesting holes to collect eggs or squabs or to shovel out droppings, whatever job it is I'm doing that day. Their feathers ruffle, they can be rough sometimes. But I don't mind my hands being pecked at, their beaks nicking my skin. I'm gentle with them, holding their wings, body and all so I can stroke their heads. They like the massage of my thumb. They're untrusting, these pigeons, but they soon stop struggling and I feel the burr of their beating hearts, the hot tremble of their bodies.

2.

The rector follows me down to the cottage, knocks on my door in that soft-knuckled way of his. He brings salted butter from the dairy, a book he wants to read to me, or some other thing. He brings me these gifts, excuses they are, and I offer him a cup of tea, a bite of bread. The loaf is wrapped in cloth to keep it fresh from weevils; they get in everything if I'm not careful.

He's pale-skinned this rector, a book man, but as much a man as any other. Only more afraid of it. I have to lift my skirts, lick my hand to make myself wet for him. He's not one for touching me beforehand, doesn't like me to look at him either. I lean against the table or press my hands down onto the seat of a chair while he takes me from behind. Holding my hips, never rough, only apologetic. I feel his little trembles, the way he tries to hold it all in, and I wish he would let go more for both our sakes.

He wipes himself on a handkerchief after and doesn't look at me. I want to hold him to my breasts, want him to stroke and kiss me. His wetness slides from between my legs, reminding me how it felt when I was loved once.

3.

I sit in the cobbled yard with a cage of panicking birds. Axe sharpened against the whetstone, woodblock stained with years of pigeon blood. My husband used to do the culling, but it's down to me now. I take a bird from the cage, feeling it quiver in my hands. I whisper words of regret, stroke its head with my thumb, then do it quickly. Lay its head on the block and sever it with one blow. I flinch with each thud of the axe. But still I hold the bird firm in my hand to stop it twitching, spraying me with its blood.

Uncertainty

Perhaps everyday will be like this: hail slicing up the sunlight as I walk through freeze until my hands burn.

Sometimes I catch myself down streets, high rises staring at me with their dim lights and cracked sliding windows. I walk with hands buried deep in my pockets and the world is a frown cutting into my forehead.

I will stop at the pedestrian crossing. I will clutch tight onto my mobile while lads in hoodies pedal past on their mountain bikes. I will laugh at myself when they're gone, curbed smiles on their faces.

Even so, it's fair to be cautious. I know people who've been mugged for less than this, their spare change rolling in the back-splash of rush hour traffic, arms protecting heads from tarmac as they watch another set of alloys slush through puddles, neon-blue lights winking at them from the back of a spoiler.

Is there a word to describe that feeling when an incident we only imagined doesn't happen? Like when we thought our mum was never coming home and, knotted up inside, we imagined bus wrecks or IRA bombs or a robbery at the post office.

And then she did walk in: tears running down her umbrella, rain spits on her glasses and her soaked-through skirt sticking to her skin.

Teaching his Daughter to Swim

He holds her level, while she kicks out with bare feet. Brown water stirred up by her splashing, dead leaves floating on the surface. These are messages that the year is almost over, and her childhood, and this moment where he can feel her goose-pimpled arms still reaching for him.

Sometimes she cries at night. He hears her from the dark of the landing when he's shutting out the lights. He stands outside her door, listens before opening it. She cries in her sleep and he wishes he could see what frightens her. Her dreams make her scrunch her nightdress tight in her fist.

Now she is kicking, almost swimming by herself. Her breath gasps as she struggles for air, spits out the lake. He imagines it tastes of silt, pond moss, rotting leaves: the taste of seven Octobers. He wants to let her go, see her swim her first strokes, but worries she might panic and stop kicking, her head slipping below the water.

The bank is only a stretch away, the path a few pine trees further, the house a race beyond that. He wants to swim the length of the lake so he can see her wave from the other side, hear her shout for him. He wants to take her in the rowing boat right to the middle and let the oars slip from his hands.

Today, the sun has a light greyer than the stones on the shoreline, than the stubble on his face. He closes his eyes, imagines that her dreams will hold them above water, even if he took his feet from the bottom, even if stones filled his pockets, even if she was a dead weight.

One of Us

we walked in the mulch of damp-trodden needles paths
fallen red and broken
plank bridges with moss trees swaying above us bare
and disorientating

we found one tree split open its wide wood legs splayed
cracked skin left dead

you watched as though you knew the strength it took
the breaking open of a tree
as though it was one of us

Frida

She lies on a bed of stones, bruised by feathers, worn by the turning of clock hands. Her forehead is creased with troubled sleep, her mouth twitching the beginning of words. She's dreaming. Maybe of crumbling buildings or white rooms with no doors, or beds without pillows. She never remembers the details, wakes with tension in her neck, a crowded head.

She drinks tequila for breakfast in tiny shot glasses, wipes sweat from her face, and waits for her husband to bring home beads for her neck, a poem, a blood orange. He is gone a long time. She unwraps ornaments from newspaper, curls her hair in rags, pinches her cheeks to give them colour. She wishes she could split one half of her from the other – sit in out-of-town bars, soak her skin in alcohol, lie with men who have coarse stubble and rough hands. She would wrap herself in their sweat, see if her husband noticed.

Instead she rubs her skin with lychees, lets her curls tumble onto her shoulders and waits barefoot. He comes home tired, but drawn to her. He kisses her cheek then pulls back, with questions on his lips. He tells her she tastes of lost summers and a trip to the beach once when they were first lovers.

Painting Natasha

When I close my eyes the brush is a violin bow, the space between us four sides of a canvas. I am painting you and wait for you to be still, hold you in arms filled with oil-stained sable brushes.

We are part of a juniper tree, the berries are whores, the leaves are blankets and we are one branch next to another. Call me sister, you say and we rest our backs against a skyless floor.

Eight years I was here, you tell me. Don't paint the scratches on my arms or my oil-slick eyes. Paint me as I should have been.

Salt and Vinegar Passion

Saturday love on the brink
of ruining me, wanting more
than a kiss in the bus shelter, more
than a fumble in a back seat:

chaos and casual lies,
drunk wrestling in a party of coats
twists and tangles of hair
and fingers and feet;

nights wrapped up
in lager-stained kisses
the scratching of each other's scars
in early hours back streets;

that slow rub into Sunday mornings
dawn pulling on eyelids,
life sliding into a cycle
of chip paper imprints.

Morning After

Hundreds of dead crickets
lie on the ground, tiny unstrung kites
their wings the edges of paper lanterns.

We wonder if weed-killer caught them
by the dusk of their throats, or maybe
sand blew in with night rain
lashing the shells from their backs.

You sweep them onto a shovel with
an outdoor brush, bristles churring
memories of wings rubbing together.

I watch you spill them into the dustbin
husks scratching on the shovel edge,
but the wind lifts them into the air,
and they scatter back across the paving.

Russian Doll

inspired by Geraldine Green's poem
~ Sulphur Beach

I was the only Russian doll he ever knew. Found in his attic, hidden under scratched records, an umbrella with bent spokes and a jigsaw with five pieces missing.

I was the one he talked to. He told me how he wanted to kick off his work shoes, slip his feet into thick socks, boots and crampons. He wanted to feel his eyelashes frost with snow, tears freeze on his cheeks, and his toes deaden from climbing mountains higher than he could imagine. He told me he wished he could find a woman who might listen to him as I did.

He wiped dust from my Russian dress. The patterns were faded, my face worn, the scar deep around my belly. I wanted him to touch my scar. I wanted him to know the doll inside me, who slept on Alessandra's pillow listening to her sob for her lover; the doll inside her who watched a surgeon pick a bullet from her lover's stomach; the doll inside her who felt the monsoon wind of his last breath. I wanted him to know the doll inside *her*, inside *her* and the smallest doll inside, the last one.

I was the only Russian doll he ever knew, the one he twisted apart at night.

Eyelashes

My wife whose eyelashes are children's first letters

~ Andre Breton

Her eyelashes are children's first letters, the uncertain curl of pencil marks along her eyelids, almost like lead pressed too hard against paper, scratched into skin.

They aren't neat or mascara'd the same way as other girls', but wayward, lost, scattering shadows across her cheeks.

They remind me of spiders' legs, tangled rug fringes, the tines of a comb.

Her eyelashes are broken letters drawn with an unsteady hand. I remember when they first brushed against me, learning to write first sentences, then paragraphs.

Me, You and the Car

He calls you names. Sweetheart. Darling. Princess. He tells you he calls his daughter Princess. Sweetcakes. Honey. Queen. Love. Pet. Flower. He says it without being sleazy. A father-daughter thing. The more he says it, the more you like it. Nobody else speaks to you like that.

He asks you questions and soon, you're the one talking, talking, talking. You sit outside the house, in his car with the engine running, but all you can hear is your own voice running away with itself, as if you might never get the chance to talk again.

You watch his creased forehead in the burn of the streetlamp. His serious stubble face. Sometimes you lose track of how many minutes pass. Other times you watch the dashboard clock, working out how long you can get away with talking, how far you can push it. You find it difficult to get out of his car those nights. Sitting in the passenger seat, hand on the door handle knowing you have to open it, but thinking not yet, not yet.

He says, always ask for me when you ring for a taxi.

You say, I don't want anybody else.

You find yourself making up imaginary visits so he will come for you. Always wanting him to take the long way round. Wanting him to lose his way so he can radio in, say he's missed his next fare.

In a lay-by opposite the all night café you drink coffee from polystyrene cups and eat bacon sandwiches. You sit in the car so nobody else can overhear you. Nobody else can see.

It was the Quiet

after the rain stopped pattering on the porch roof and the day broke, sun slipping for the first time through grey, a damp where nobody left their houses in case it started again

after she saw everyone off to school and work, feet clattering down the stairs, books in bags, briefcases, pockets filled with keys and coins and handkerchiefs

when the door shut to, car doors, tail lights disappearing from view

Autumn
Sundays
early mornings before her family were awake
the rising of bread dough or scones
crisscross of the cooling tray

it was small sounds, the post landing on the mat, electric hum of the milk float, bottles clinking

the plumping of cushions
folding of sheets
matching odd socks in the emptiness of bedrooms
when everyone was out

there was even something about lying in the sour grey of a sickbed
hum whisper a tongue a mouth a lipstick rub on a forehead leaning over to say something she never heard

trees rustling their leaves outside
sockfall in the hallway
a *sh quiet she's asleep*

it was the way she used to breathe, almost as if she wasn't breathing
not this *rasp rasp* sandpaper noise she now made

Writing the Weather

for ST

I always write about rain
the way drizzle soaks through clothes and clings every inch to my skin
or gushing rain, drumming against the porch roof, bay window, car windscreen when the wipers are struggling

I've never written about hail
how driving down the Oldham Road, hailstone fists beat down on the bonnet, and the girl I was with cowered, brought her hands over her face
not like she thought hail might rip through metal, I think it was the sound she was afraid of
as if it was a sound she'd heard before, fists banging against a door, boots kicking at the wall, a fighting noise, a noise louder than her own voice or thoughts

sometimes I write about grey skies, they make me think of her
sun breaking through
a sunset of cuts along her arms
lips white, so long pressed together

Nights With You

these nights in a bar, these nights watching you, the strings of your guitar cutting into your skin, these nights talking, conversations tilting your way then my way, wanting something, not sure whether it's the same thing

these nights in the front room of your ground floor flat, all the noises from outside cutting in, listening to this city scratching at the door, this way of living

wondering if we might meet in an underpass, walk past our own graffiti feelings sprayed onto walls, too scared to read them, after nights alone, nights colder than we'd known

Last Night

Last night, a helicopter sliced the air with machete blades, chasing stolen cars. Its noise angry, circling away then back again. I didn't hear the screech of tyres as I sometimes do. It was almost midnight. The noise cut into my sleep, it unsettled me.

Last night, I jemmied the window of a car, snapped the steering lock. I turned a screwdriver in the cap. It didn't start, but I remember driving it.

Last night, I had a gun to my head. I recognised the man with his finger on the trigger. He pulled it and click. No bullet.

This morning I woke to a black feather on my pillow, the quill cut my fingers when I touched it. I woke with one blink of my eyes like something had startled me, a moth behind the curtains maybe, a noise, the flap of wings or a memory.

Chasing Invisible Things

far away sea
wind so cold I wrap my cardigan tight   fasten the toggles
on my coat

further on
a boy picks up string and seaweed   rocks and tin cans
turns them over in his fingers   reading them   spinning and
twirling them   inspecting them   his eyes searching for the
next one

always five steps behind   a girl chases him
wind blowing hair into her face   scarf loosening and twist-
curving down the beach   turquoise and green   billowing away
as if it too is chasing something

boy chasing carrier bags chasing a scarf chasing a girl
chasing a boy chasing invisible things

my feet stamp footprints into the beach   the sea
fills them with brown sand lakes

Lightning Source UK Ltd.
Milton Keynes UK
28 November 2009

146846UK00001B/67/A

9 780905 127132